IMAGES
of England

YATE

Trent House in Station Road was built in the 1900s by Joseph Hall for his retirement, after many years as the station master. Mr and Mrs Hall and their three daughters, together with 'Prince' the pony, can be seen in front of the house. The building was pulled down in the 1980s to make way for the present Esso petrol station.

IMAGES
of England

YATE

Compiled by
The Yate District Oral History Project

TEMPUS

First published 1998
Copyright © The Yate District Oral History Project, 1998

Tempus Publishing Limited
The Mill, Brimscombe Port,
Stroud, Gloucestershire, GL5 2QG

ISBN 0 7524 1523 9

Typesetting and origination by
Tempus Publishing Limited
Printed in Great Britain by
Midway Clark Printing, Wiltshire

Front cover: Workers in the courtyard of Stanshawes Court, *c.* 1920. They have just installed a new heating system in the house. Each man has a flower in his buttonhole and is holding a different item relating to the installation of the system.

In the laundry garden in the early 1920s. Mr Frank Iles and his wife, Ruth, are in the garden of the laundry that serviced Poole Court. The building was in Station Road in the vicinity of the present ambulance station, opposite Carlton House.

Contents

Council workmen before the First World War with their steam traction engine, carrying a load of stone from the nearby quarry. Rufus Nelson (seated) steered and Fred Watts drove the traction engine.

Acknowledgements

The following people or organisations were kind enough to loan or donate material, give advice and/or assist in other ways during the preparation of this book:

Geoff Adams, Glenys Anderson, Mabel Ayres, Howard Beard, David Brace, Sheila and John Bullock, Verdun Cater, John Cox, George Davey, Joan Davis, Audrey Dolman, Jim Elsworth, Mrs S. England, *The Evening Post*, Joan Febry, *The Gazette*, General Domestic Appliances Ltd, Tink and Marjorie Gibbins, Mrs G. Higgins, Ruby Hart, Mr D. Holbrook, Maurice Horder, Mary Isaac, Sheila Jabs, Bob Jordan, Alan Marshall, Anthony Masters and Associates, Lynda and Barry Miller, Mr and Mrs Mulchinock, Gladys Nelson, Pearl Perry, Steve Potter, Maurice Rudge, Colin Sluter, Mr Snartt, Universal Pictorial Press and Agency, R. Kingsley Tayler, The Tozer Collection, Les Walters, R. Will, Janet Williams, Peter Williams, Bernard and Kathleen Wooles, Yate Heritage Centre.

Introduction

For some years now, the Yate District Oral History Project has been involved in the collation of recordings and photographs for its archives. The evidence that has been gathered very much reflects the changes in the community over a period of many decades. It became increasingly apparent that this wealth of photographic material, supplemented by personal memories, very much merited publication. A tremendous resource has also been found in the vast collection of postcards, with their accompanying messages, that have generously been loaned to us. Many of the postcards used photographs taken by Murray Dowding at the beginning of the twentieth century, without whom we would know much less about life in those days.

The Project, fired by enthusiasm, embarked upon this undertaking in order to share its recollections of yesteryear with others. Undoubtedly, this would include many who have lived in Yate all their lives, but also new residents who would equally value an insight into its past.

We have photographs that show buildings and roads of yesteryear, many of which changed with the coming of the railways and the motor car. There is also material showing the fairs, fêtes, sports days and outings – which were usually centred around the churches, chapels and the grand houses. Many of the traditional workplaces recorded in this compilation, such as the colliery, the dye-works and the sawmills, have long since gone, only to be taken over by industrial warehousing and light industry. From our selection of photographs we can gain an insight into fashion – from the elegance of the Victorian and Edwardian ladies to the everyday dress of working men and women and the austerity of wartime uniforms. Once, small businesses and shops contributed to everyday life and there was always time to talk. Very few are left, the focus now being in the modern shopping centre. Pockets of rural Yate still remain but the new town has seen the disappearance of the livestock market, the abattoir, the blacksmiths and many other crafts associated with an agricultural community.

It is surprising, with the rapid development of recent years, that no new schools were built until 1954 to augment St Mary's School (The National School) and North Road School (The British School). Since this time, many primary schools and two secondary schools have been established to meet the needs of the growing community.

What can we learn by reflecting upon the evidence published within these pages? Henry Ford once said, 'History is more or less bunk'. How wrong he certainly was, living as we do in a world where the pace of change is far more rapid than our ancestors could have visualised. Now, it is more important than ever that we have a deepening interest in the past. Nostalgic we may be, but without that knowledge we cannot begin to understand the present, yet alone contemplate a future which will be vastly different from our own.

If we look back at Yate over the twentieth century, we realise that we live very much in a materialistic world. Social and economic changes have seen the passing of family shops, many pubs, the village schools, the doctors' surgeries, the farms, mines and the country lanes as our grandparents and their grandparents knew them. In a world where poverty, unemployment and illness were an ever-present threat, they seemingly enjoyed a contented and peaceful existence where family bonds were all-important. This is why it is so vital to reflect upon the past. If our forebears received only a very elementary form of education, they nevertheless can teach us so much about life and how to live it in a rapidly moving world.

In the compilation of this book we have made every effort to be accurate in processing the information gained from numerous sources. If, however, any errors are apparent, we trust that you will bear with us. So much material was loaned to us that it was impossible to use all of it. We would like to express our sincere thanks to all those who loaned us material and our regret that it was not possible to include all of it in this book.

We have compiled the contents of the book from material in the YDOHP archives and enhanced this with photographs and picture postcards kindly loaned to us. The latter were published in abundance during the early part of the twentieth century and have provided a wealth of information. Details on the backs of some of the cards have given us, for example: dates, weather conditions, train arrival times and messages of a more mysterious nature.

We hope that this book of Yate of yesteryear will be of great interest to both the older and new residents of the town. It will no doubt be a source of discussion and maybe more photographs and anecdotes will come to light.

YDOHP is an historical society, established in 1987, whose aim is to record the ever-changing face of Yate. Their archive is housed in Yate Library and manned by volunteers who progress the work of the Project. There are also monthly open meetings at Poole Court when members of the Project and visitors come to listen to a variety of interesting talks by local historians.

Foreword

The Bible is full of story telling. The Community of God retells its history of famous events, the disasters, the heroes and the common folk of the past, all reinforcing the uniqueness of this special community. In this way the past is handed on and the current community grows as it journeys on. The Yate Oral History Project are the modern successors to this inheritance and tradition. We are grateful to them.

They have told and provided photographs for this visual age which show the development of Yate from a small village with its church and market, its blacksmith and workhouse, through the glories of Parnall's and Newman's to the modern town, which is still growing, with its churches, shopping centre, leisure facilities, much light industry and many schools.

In the heart of this new town, there are a variety of small communities and neighbourhoods where the history is remembered, retold and passed on. The old buildings are preserved and form part of that history and life goes on and grows on. In a mobile population there is a deep desire for roots and a sense of belonging and for a history from which we have come. This helps us settle and belong and decide where we want to be. Yate is a good place to be, to live, and enjoy living.

The Revd David Sutch
Rector

One
Buildings and Views

The Swan Inn, outside which a fine selection of cars are parked, 1930s. On the left of the picture, a wall can be seen where Joyce Webb, later Mrs Gray, once had a hairdressing salon. On the right is the blacksmith's shop.

The ruins of Yate Court, on the way to Rangeworthy. The Court was occupied by Roundheads during the Civil War, in around 1640. Fearing for the safety of these men, Colonel Massey came from Gloucester to relieve the small garrison. When they were ready to leave, they made sure that the Court would be of no use to the Royalists and turned their cannons on the building. Only the gatehouse remained, along with a few sturdy walls.

The gatehouse of Yate Court, c. 1920. This is an idyllic photograph of Mr and Mrs Bradridge, who owned Yate Court Farm, and Eileen Pritchard, from Lattimer Farm, by the gatehouse of Yate Court. The gatehouse once contained the portcullis, which was dismantled and taken to Berkeley in around 1910. Following the destruction by the Roundheads, the Court never recovered and continued as a homestead farm. Eileen Pritchard appears again later in this book (on page 77, as Eileen Weaver), albeit in a somewhat different position.

Stanshawes Court. Squire Hooper, as he was known, bought the Stanshawes Estate in 1874. Here he built the Court, two lodges for the gardeners, a cottage for his groom and coachman and two cottages, known as Duckmead, for the laundry workers. He also landscaped extensive gardens and established two farms. Mr Hooper enjoyed showing off his estate by holding fêtes and grand parties. A band would always be in attendance at these events.

The head gardener's cottage. The two lodges, at the end of the drive at Stanshawes Court, were built for Squire Hooper's head gardener, Mr Walters, and his assistant. Four further gardeners were employed as there was much work in tending the kitchen garden, the hothouses and the vinery, not to mention the extensive formal gardens.

Around the lake at Stanshawes. There were lakes on each side of the driveway, close to the Court, where the swans and wild ducks made their homes. Peacocks could be seen strutting on the lawns during the late 1800s.

A photograph taken from the Lodge window. In each of the lodges was a small window, one facing up the drive and one facing down. There was a gate across the drive and it was the duty of the gardener's wife to make sure that she ran out to open it to allow Squire Hooper's carriage to go through.

The stables at Stanshawes Court. Squire Hooper was a keen huntsman and this photograph, from around 1910, shows the stables and the groom's cottages at the back. Above this grew a huge vine, which required great attention from the gardeners.

Poole Court was built in the early 1850s. It was occupied by the Hills, a well-known Bristol shipping family, until the First World War. During the war it was used as an officers' mess by the Royal Flying Corps and, in 1925, was acquired by George Parnall & Company. In 1932, it was sold to the Newman brothers, Augustus and Hedley, and it became part of their industrial complex until the late 1980s. By then it was in a poor state of repair and was in danger of being demolished by developers of the Newman's site. It was bought by Yate Town Council for £1 in 1990 and completely refurbished. It has proved to be a great asset to the town, being used as the Yate Town Council Offices, the Registry Office and the meeting place for various groups and associations, including the Yate District Oral History Project and the Yate Heritage Centre.

The Ridge House, *c.* 1912. This was the home of Colonel Burges who, with his daughters, supported the Baden Powell movement and started troupes in Chipping Sodbury. Unfortunately, this lovely house was demolished in the 1970s and the site is now occupied by ARC offices.

The lodge to The Ridge House. This cottage can still be seen in Station Road, opposite the old workhouse. The drive was lined with walnut trees leading to the 'big house'. At one time, Mr Slade was the gardener and was working in this capacity up to the time that the house was demolished in the 1970s. After this he continued to use the gardens to grow flowers and vegetables for his own business.

Yate House, which was built in the early 1700s. This lovely Georgian mansion, in Gravel Hill Road, is now known as Rockwood House. For generations it was owned by the Randolph family who held both the Brinsham and Yate Manors. After the death of William Cater Randolph in 1898 it passed to his son, Henry de Beaumont Randolph, who eventually sold it in 1911 to William and Richard Fox. The sale took place on 2 August 1911 at the Portcullis Hotel in Chipping Sodbury. Since then it has been a hotel and a nightclub, besides standing empty for some years. It has now been extended and converted into flats.

Yate Rectory, near St Mary's church, early 1900s. It was wrongly known as Poole Court from the time when it was occupied by Hedley Newman during the 1950s or 1960s. Rectors who lived in the Rectory could walk to the churchyard along a grove of lime trees and over a footbridge (across the River Frome) without going along the main road. The iron gate at the end of the grove is still in place. This building was demolished in the early 1980s to make way for the development of Canterbury Close.

Yate Rectory Gardens, *c.* 1909. The gardens ran down to the River Frome, which in those days could be used for boating, and contained a blue-tiled swimming pool and fir trees. Care had to be taken to avoid the waterfall adjacent to the garden. The pool was filled in as part of later development but some of the trees are still there, and are now of a substantial height.

Yate Rectory, in what is now Canterbury Close, *c.* 1930. This was built in the 1920s to replace the earlier rectory. Sadly, Canon E.R. Smith committed suicide here in 1933. The building has now been converted into two flats with a new, smaller rectory being built nearby in Canterbury Close.

The Cottage Hospital, opened by the trustees of the local War Memorial Fund in 1920, using the funds which then stood at £2,000. It was initially called the Chipping Sodbury and District War Memorial Hospital and served all the surrounding villages who had contributed to the War Memorial Fund. A plaque was displayed in the main hall, giving the names of the men who died in the First World War. Originally the hospital, situated in Station Road opposite the junction with Broadway, had been a private house – known as Melrose House in around 1830. The earliest known resident was J.T. Coryton. The hospital continued after 1948 under the National Health Service, but ceased functioning on 5 November 1988. It is currently used as a clinic for the mentally and physically disabled.

The back and front of Yate Lawns, c. 1910. Now known as the Lawns Hotel, this was once owned by Mr E.A. Hitchens. Once a year, he took apples from his extensive orchards – carried in large baskets by his gardener Mr Walters – across the green to St Mays's School. Here, pupils paraded past to choose two apples each. Some of the boys knew which were the sweetest apples to select, as they had been in the orchard before!

The Turnpike which stood on the Chipping Sodbury to Wickwar road at the junction of Love Lane. This was demolished in the early 1970s. Mrs Hawkins (née Fanny Iles), the daughter of a well-known Yate family who taught at the National School (now St Mary's), lived there in the 1900s. It was the home of Miss Anstey in the 1930s.

The first Council building in Yate was built in around 1896 for £150, using subscriptions from local people. It was used for meetings and located next to the old Baptist chapel opposite the White Lion public house on the site of the present ambulance station. Both buildings were demolished in the 1960s to make way for a road-widening scheme. It was used as the Parish Hall until October 1934 when the new hall, built by Mr Lemon, was opened. From 1934 the old hall was used for many purposes, including a reading room, a greengrocer's, a fish shop and by the Women's Institute. It was sold to the District Council, in the early 1980s, for £2,000.

Cottage opposite The Swan public house and the forge in Station Road. This was once lived in by Mr and Mrs Higgins and is where their son was born. Later, it was occupied by Miss Hale. On the left, beyond the cottage, can just be seen Snepps Cottage where, in the early 1900s, Colonel Snepp and his family lived. Later, Dr Davies and his family resided there. The site is currently used by The Willows Nursing Home.

Cottages in The Barton, which was the area opposite the White Lion. The cottages were demolished when the shopping centre was built and were on the open space leading into the centre. Residents in the cottages have included Ernest May, Mrs Fry, Mr and Mrs Randall Horder, Mr and Mrs Moore and Mr and Mrs Boulton, whose son George died of diptheria. The larger house on the right was occupied by Mr and Mrs Jarrett.

Jesmond Dene in Station Road (opposite Safeway), about to be demolished at the time that the shopping centre was being built. Mrs Taylor formerly lived in Jesmond Dene. Mrs Fletcher's cottage and cycle shop next door had already been demolished by the time that this photograph was taken. The house adjoining Jesmond Dene was Poole View, where Mr and Mrs H. Nelson lived.

Roadside cottages opposite Ridgewood. These little cottages survived until the 1970s, when they were demolished and houses built in their gardens. The large building on the right is Firgrove House, which is now a nursing home. For many years it had belonged to Major David Brown and his family.

Aerial view of the junction of Station Road and Church Road, before the building of the shopping centre, 1960s. A careful look will identify many of the buildings and areas mentioned elsewhere in this book. Note the prefabs in Lawns Road, which have long since been demolished. At the end of this road, opposite the entrance to St Mary's church, is what was once the Yate village green but has now been partially built upon.

Thorn's Farm. This seventeenth-century farmhouse was occupied by the Thorners prior to 1784 and it was from this family name that it became known as Thorn's Farm. It was owned by a succession of farmers up until the late 1960s, when Sodbury District Council purchased it. The building was then used as a community centre until it was demolished prior to development. The area is currently occupied by the Magistrate's Court and Thorn's Farm Close. A monkey puzzle tree, which originates from the original farm garden, is still there today.

Brinshan or Brimsham Farm, just north of the junction of Gravel Hill Road and the Wickwar Road. This building replaced Brinsham Manor during Tudor times. Courts were held here, usually every six months, presided over by the lord of the manor. This photograph shows the oldest part of the farm; the window on the downstairs right looks into the panelled courtroom.

Warren Farm (now demolished) was near the old cattle market and adjacent to the railway line in North Road where part of the Jordan Group is now sited. On the left is Elaine Little and on the right is her sister, Gwen Little. Their father was the stationmaster in around 1920.

Rectory Farm (now demolished) is the site of the development in the vicinity of Wellington Road off Greenways Road. The farm was originally part of the manor of the rectory of Yate, rents being paid to the bounty of Queen Anne and, later, to the church commission. The house was probably Elizabethan.

Goose Green Farm in the early 1900s. This farmhouse is still to be found by the roundabout junction of Goose Green Way and Randolph Avenue. The farmlands used to stretch northwards towards Leechpool Farm, but are now in the process of being developed. The house is difficult to date precisely, but it appears to have been in existence during the first half of the seventeenth century, when it was inhabited by members of the Neale family. Over the years, as is common in old houses, many alterations and additions have taken place. Some very early wall paintings have been uncovered during refurbishment works.

Partridge Farm, demolished in the late 1980s, is now the site of Partridge Close. It was occupied by John Russell in 1784 and, later, by the Cox family. The last residents were the Bailey family.

The back of Elmgrove Farm, which was built in around 1890 (now demolished), and the site of the former Heron offices and Elmgrove Drive. Mr Willy Werrett is next to the caravan with his wife and daughter-in-law. The pigsty and slaughterhouse can also be seen. Earlier occupants of the farm were George Carter and his wife in 1927 and the Hill family, who subsequently moved to the cottage by the Lawns – which is now The Funky Forest play area. Mr Boulton, the headmaster of St Mary's School, also lived in the farm from 1934 until 1963 (in preference to the damp schoolhouse).

A farm labourer and a lady, who has just fetched water from the spring, make their way home, early 1900s. The only source of water for Yate Rocks was from this one spring.

Yate Rock, early 1900s. Besides the cottages, there had been a small general shop and a Baptist chapel (which closed in 1971).

Yate Rocks, looking over the rustic bridge by the ford. Apparently, the writer of the card bought rabbits from the cottage marked 'X', during the early 1900s.

The Spike was the common name for the workhouse, built in around 1837 to conform with the Poor Law Act of 1834. The Spike was, in fact, the pointed tower above the workhouse. It was destroyed in 1928 by a fire that had begun in the roof of the master's quarters and it was never replaced.

Miss Sybil Moreton is leaning on the gate outside her parents' home in Station Road, 1920s. The property was later demolished and the site occupied by a petrol station opposite to Parnalls' Gate near Sunnyside Lane. Mr Moreton sold boots and shoes from a shop in Chipping Sodbury.

The original YMCA in Station Road, which was in use in the early 1900s. The building later became a butcher's shop, owned by Mr Charratt, a well-known character in the village.

The new YMCA memorial stone ceremony on 1 July 1916. The new building in Station Road was donated by the Fox family of Yate House for the youth of the parish. It is currently being used by a nursery group.

Station Road in the 1900s. This postcard was postmarked on 29 April 1907 and the message reads 'Bitter cold weather and heavy rains'.

Station Road, early 1900s. A lovely tranquil scene with the carriage and horses coming round the bend.

Horse and cart in Station Road. These were still the main means of transport at the beginning of the twentieth century. Note the shops on the left and the Coach Inn to the right of the picture.

Travelling along towards the station in 1903, a bystander poses for the photograph.

Truly Rural Station Road, 3 March 1914, although many locals knew it as Yate Road. Opposite the horse and cart is the turning into Eggshill Lane. The two children appear to have the grass verge to themselves.

Station Road looking east, between the wars. Notice the airfield on the left.

Aerial view of Station Road, looking west towards Nibley, early 1970s. Much was about to change, with the development of the shopping centre and the demolition of Newman's in the foreground. In the background are the Parnall's factory and the airfield – which is now a housing estate.

An empty Westerleigh Road during the 1930s. This would be a very different picture today!

North Road before widening, near the junction with Mission Road, *c.* 1977. These old cottages had to be demolished to make way for the progress of the motor car.

Picture postcard to remind you of St Mary's church, the railway station, Stanshawes Court and Poole Court, early 1900s.

Two
Churches and Chapels

St Mary's church before 1897. The transept walls are Norman but most of the building dates from the fourteenth and fifteenth centuries. The tower is Perpendicular and is, at this time, without its cresting.

St Mary's church, 1897. Work is being carried out on the tower to add cresting to commemorate Queen Victoria's Diamond Jubilee.

The Revd James Madden Ford, who served as rector of St Mary's church for twenty-six years, from 1896-1922. He was a very popular clergyman.

Choirboys outside St Mary's church, July 1933. From left to right, back row: Peter Smoothy, Harold Slade, Wilfred Smoothy, Tink Gibbons, Alfred Howell. Middle row: Jack Brain, George Strange, Herbert Strange, Alan Lanham. Front row: Leslie Griffiths, Gordon Cryer, Gordon Edwards, John Williams, John Cox.

The tower of St Mary's church. This is ninety-two feet high and has a peal of six bells. The smallest is the treble and was a gift from Richard Stokes, of Stanshawes Court, in 1723.

The interior of St Mary's church before the modernisation when the pulpit and pews were removed. The window above the High Altar was given by five Pontifex brothers in memory of their father, Edmund. The organ is Victorian, near to which the two Fox brothers sat in the pews for church services.

'Appeal for a Peal', 1930s. A sum of £250 was needed to re-hang the bells in a metal frame. Members of the church sold squares at one shilling each to reach this target. This was accomplished and the bells re-hung in 1931. This collecting card was on the back of the postcard of St Mary's church tower (opposite).

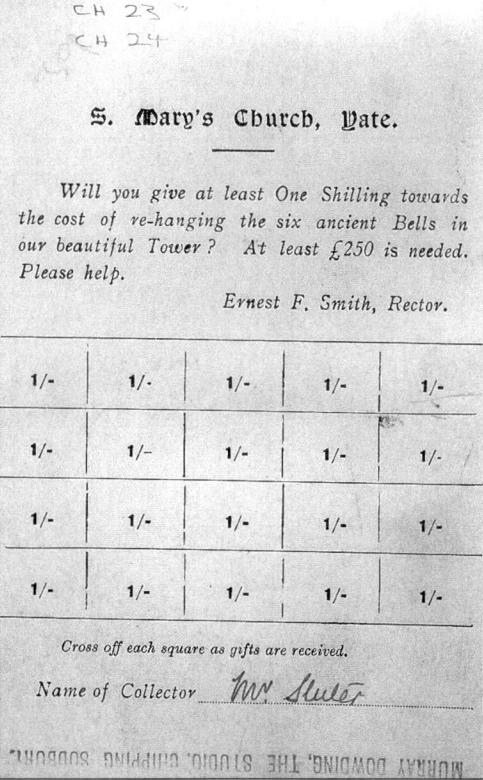

An aerial view of St Mary's church and school. Taken in the early 1900s, the school garden can be seen where the new St Mary's School, built in 1966, now stands. Note the Lawns Hotel, The White Lion and the barn.

The nine handbell ringers from St Mary's church, c. 1900. From left to right are: Fred Coombs, Sidney Cox, William Pride, Sam Bowyers, Percy Hopkins, Bert Haynes, Joe Warner, Reg Iles, Percy Iles.

Later handbell ringers from St Mary's church, c. 1930. This group played in the homes of elderly people each Christmas and also in the grand houses. From left to right, back row: Tom Curtis, -?-, Harold Hulands, Sid Nelson, Wilf Taylor, -?-, George Gowen, Gilbert Iles. Front row: -?-, Hugh Nelson, Len White, -?- and Frank Fletcher.

St Mary's church from the Newman's Sports Field adjacent to Poole Court, after the First World War. This view is no longer there, as the area has now been developed for housing.

Yate Mothers' Union, 7 October 1929 from St Mary's church. They are all in hats outside the Mission Road church, off North Road, with the rector – the Revd Foster Morris – and his wife. In the picture are: Mrs Fletcher, Mrs May, Mrs Alway, Mrs Pritchard, Mrs Andrews, Mrs Washen, Mrs Gunstan, Mrs Dando, Mrs Wookey, Mrs Watkins, Mrs Powell, Mrs Dyer, Mrs Cook, Mrs Lomas, Mrs Hendy, Mrs Reeves, Mrs Nelson, Mrs Strange, Mrs Dixon, Mrs Deardon, Mrs Webb and Mrs Mainstone.

The North Road tin Baptist chapel, *c.* 1900. This was replaced in 1909 with the present stone building. The tin chapel was eventually pushed (approximately 200 yards) up the road on rollers to the home of Mr A. Pearce, who used it as a shed for many years.

The first wedding at North Road Baptist chapel, opposite Mission Road, on 29 May 1939. This took place thirty years after the chapel had been built. The wedding was between Ken Prout and Ilene Holbrook. The bridesmaids are, from left to right: Dorothy Thompson, Valerie Guy, Mavis Holbrook and Sybil Holbrook. The pastor, at the back on the right, is Arthur Britton.

Members of North Road Baptist chapel, 1920s. The gentleman with the beard in the centre of the second row is 'Gaffer' Rogers, headmaster of the North Road British School, who was very much involved with the chapel. To the left of Mr Rogers is Mabel Dyer (née Cook), who was the organist for many years. On her right is Seth Dyer, one of the founder members of the North Road Baptist chapel.

The remains of Hope Congregational church in Stover Road. It was well used during the 1930s for services and weddings. It closed in 1958 due to lack of support and was demolished in the late 1960s.

A tea party at Hope 'chapel'. In the picture are: Lisa Batten, Reg Batten, Doreen Gingell, Mrs Rowlands, Reg Ballam, Esther Batten, Dennis Roland, Mrs George Curtis, Mrs White, Betty Davis, Jose Ballam, Susan Ballam (child), Mary Fox, and Mr Tanner.

Three
Transport

Wheel bier, or carriage, for transporting coffins to their last resting place. This one was purchased by the parish of Yate in 1901 and is currently displayed in the foyer of Poole Court.

Horse and carriage, *c.* 1900. Mr Perrett, the coachman to the Revd J.M. Ford, is outside the Rectory Lodge. Judging by the snow on the ground and the trees, it appears to be rather cold.

Yate railway station was opened in 1854 and was on the south side of the road bridge, rather than the north (where the present station is sited). A short distance to the north of the old station is the branch line to Thornbury, which opened on 2 September 1872. The old station house and the combined goods and engine shed are still in use today, but are no longer part of the railway complex. Both structures were designed by Brunel and the goods shed is now a listed building.

Staff at Yate station, with the station house in the background, *c.* 1900.

Staff at Yate railway station before the First World War. This group includes Mr Baker, the stationmaster. The question of wages was to cause concern over the coming years. In 1914 the average wage was twenty-nine shillings (£1.45) per week, rising to a zenith of seventy-eight shillings (£3.90) in 1921 but falling to fifty-eight shillings (£2.90) in 1922. These figures come from the diary of George Bacon (see page 99). He also comments on the problems of snowdrifts on the line.

Yate Station, *c.* 1920. The train is arriving to take passengers on a day's excursion.

The Midland Flyer, seen here passing through Yate Station in 1920. Note the turntable in front of the goods and engine shed, which was in a cramped position between the foot and road bridges.

Oh Dr Beeching! Yate Station was closed to passengers in January 1965 and completely closed in December 1967. Only through trains used the line from that time onwards. Mr Fear and his daughter witness the last train leave. A new station was eventually opened on 11 May 1989.

Yate Methodist church outing, 1924. Included in this picture are: Mrs and Mrs Harold Cox, Mr and Mrs Bacon and their son, Cyril, Mrs Shellard from Walnut Cottage, Mrs Shellard's brother-in-law (who was a lay preacher), Mr and Mrs Lemon (Mr Lemon was a builder) Mrs Gertrude Higgins, Violet Lemon and Mr and Mrs Stagg with their daughter, Vera.

Station Road garage forecourt in the 1950s, with Mr Charlie Pullin, who owned the garage, on the left. The young lad on the motor bike is Gerald Virgo and the other lad is believed to be a mechanic employed by Mr Pullin. The garage and the large property known as Trent House were pulled down to make way for the present Esso petrol station.

This brand new Super Sentinel lorry has just been delivered from the factory in the Midlands, *c.* 1930. It is shown here outside Providence House in North Road. Mr J. Washbourne was a well-known haulage contractor in the Yate area.

Roadworkers who repaired the roads in Yate and Chipping Sodbury. Rufus Nelson was the driver of the steamroller, which dates from the early 1900s.

The Pearce family and their car, at the entrance of the Lawns, *c.* 1950. From left to right they are: Tom, Lewis, Edith and Elsie.

Four
Wartime

"Nine of the Nuts."

Workers from the Air Ministry Maintenance Base, known as No. 3 Aircraft Depot, stationed at Poole Court in the First World War. The original base was built by German prisoners of war in 1916 and 1917.

War-workers during the First World War, in the field behind Cow Mills, where they made grenades and other missiles in the munitions factory. From left to right, front row: Eliza Batten, Winnie Fletcher, Alice Green, Lily Cox. Back row: Annie Bond, -?- and -?-.

Soldiers at Yate station during the First World War.

Games at Poole Court, 1918. The wounded that could not take part in the sports are sitting with some of the competitors.

Ladies' tug-o'-war, RAF Sports Day, 1918. A few ladies actually managed to keep their hats on!

RAF Sports Day, 1918. Poole Court was the RAF Headquarters during the war and the event was held in the grounds. St Mary's church can be seen in the background.

The RAF depot band tuning up in the grounds of Poole Court, 1918.

No. 5 barrack room for 'The Bristol Own', *c.* 1915. This was probably on the old aerodrome.

Aircraft repairs section (ARS). The main entrance, off Station Road, was where damaged planes were brought and repaired. They included planes such as the Sopwith Pups, Sopwith Camels, Avros and Bristol Fighters. The airman standing to attention, facing the motor car, is Mr Charles Woodruff. The depot became Yate Market after the First World War.

Annie Hulands in the uniform of the Royal Flying Corps. She was the daughter of Mr and Mrs William Hulands. The Royal Flying Corps became the Royal Air Force on 1 April 1918.

During the First World War, Yate became the home of the Royal Flying Corps. A large camp was laid out on a piece of land in the Westerleigh Road, which is now Cooper's engineering factory. This was the camp's bakery.

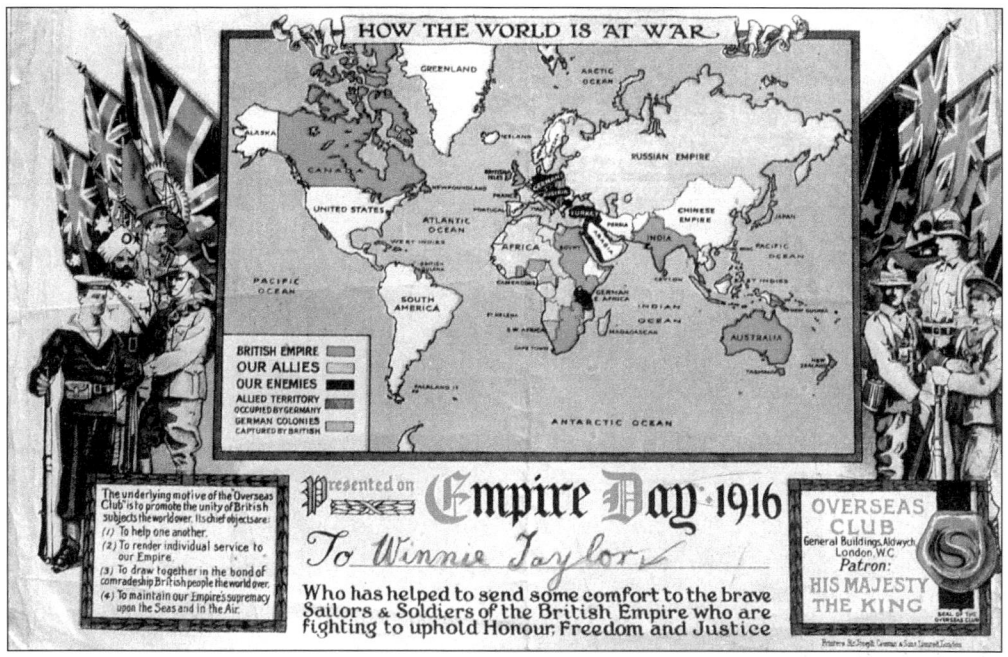

The Overseas Club was established to send some comfort to the sailors and soldiers fighting for the British Empire. This card, produced by the club on Empire Day 1916, was sent to Winnie Taylor, who lived in Yate all her life (see page 92).

Thursday 27 February 1941 was a dull and cloudy day when, in mid-afternoon, a single German Heinkel bomber machine-gunned and bombed Parnall's factory. Fifty-three personnel were killed and forty seriously injured. On Friday 7 March, the factory was bombed again and this time three people died.

A Frazer-Nash gun turret, made at Parnall's, was displayed in London's Trafalgar Square. These turrets were fitted into Lancaster and Wellington bombers. Wings For Victory was a savings campaign to encourage people to save money to help the war effort.

The Lancaster bomber displayed outside St Paul's Cathedral. The gun turrets, manufactured at Parnall's, were located at the nose, tail and on the top of the plane.

Firemen at Parnall's during the Second World War.

The large generator at
Newman's in 1942. The
generator was probably
originally purchased second-
hand and refurbished. It was
subsequently used as a stand-by
generator in case of a mains
electricity failure.

Air raid wardens at Newman's. They are wearing special gear, including rubber boots. The man sitting on the far right is Mr Mosedale, who originally came from Tewkesbury as chauffeur to Canon Smith. After the canon's death, he worked at Newman's (see page 17).

Newman's FAP during the Second World War. Second from the left in the front row is Nurse Stinchcombe, who came from Wales. On her left is the dentist Jimmy Sarafian, brother of Dr Sarafian Senior.

Queen Mary visiting the ARP ambulance station, which was on land adjacent to the community centre. This land was owned by a petrol company and surrounded by a large, green-painted, galvanised fence. She also paid a visit to Poole Court on the same day.

Queen Mary visiting Newman's industries during the Second World War, escorted by Hedley Newman. Fourth from the left in the front row is Bill Payne. Queen Mary's cavalcade was often seen passing through Yate on her way to, or from, Badminton House, where she lived during the war. She often visited Newman's during this period and her Daimler, as well as a soldier escort's motor bike, can be seen in this photograph. One of her escorts was Mr Mellor, who married Phyllis Garde, a local girl who worked at Newman's.

Queen Mary visiting Newman's canteen, with Hedley Newman, during the Second World War. Mr and Mrs Stan Jeal were in charge of the canteen, which is in the background, and it was used as a social club after the war. The woman behind the queen's lady-in-waiting, is probably Mrs A.J. Newman.

Home Guard training: staff at Newman's are taking a keen interest in what the instructor is showing them. From left to right: K. Marlow, F. Tandy, H. Cheeseman, L. Walters, Ted Hale, -?- (instructor), ? Jefferies, -?-, -?- and -?-.

Air raid shelter, 11 March 1987. The entrance to an underground shelter built in the back garden of a house in Westerleigh Road during the Second World War. The owners, Mr and Mrs Percy Garraway, came to Yate in the 1930s. Two or three members of the Yate District Oral History Project can remember some very cold nights in this shelter in the early 1940s.

The end of the Second World War in Europe and these ladies are celebrating at the home of Mr and Mrs Marquands, at 86 Westerleigh Road. Amongst the happy faces are: Mrs Kilminster, Mrs Potter, Mrs Box, Molly Jordan, Mrs Cooke, Mrs Watts, Mrs Gwen Tilling (with the jug) and Mrs Sheila Marquand (third from the left).

VE celebrations by Yate residents at the Old House in Home PH in Burton. Some of these people are: Wilf Taylor, Cyril Fry, Sid Nelson, Jumbo Boulton, S. Febry, W. Wotton, Mr and Mrs Willy and Mr E. May.

Five
Industry

Cow Mills, supplier of cattle feed, situated handily next to the Cow Inn and run by Sarah Warner, who later lived in Station Road, 1920s. Jimmy Dixon is in the cart nearest the camera. The mills used to be in the old parish of Sodbury.

Eggshill Lane Colliery, closed in 1906, is currently the site of a housing development built in around 1970 by Horace Tily. In the late 1980s, the covering to an old shaft collapsed in the garden of one of the properties and had to be filled in.

The ink works, built on the site of the old colliery in Eggshill Lane in the 1940s. This establishment closed in 1964. The works produced ochre or lead chromate, which was a pale brownish-yellow pigment used in paints and the printing of ten-shilling notes. The photograph includes Jim Williams, whose son Harold took his lunch to him every day to avoid dust contamination spoiling the food.

Blakeney's Sawmills, early 1950s. This was a thriving business at this time. The yard was situated on Westerleigh Road, opposite the junction to Eggshill Lane. It was owned by Mr Blakeney but managed by Mr Dibble, his son-in-law, and his son, Metford.

Workers at Blakeney's Sawmills, c. 1920. Tom Fletcher is second from the right in the back row. Incidents involving the circular saw were not uncommon in the days when safety was not such an important issue.

During the First World War, Robert McAlpine manufactured concrete slabs in a factory near to the railway station. This is now the site of part of the Jordan Group.

Bert Norman came from Northcreake, in Norfolk, to Chipping Sodbury in 1938. He had been apprenticed to Burrell's – the engineers at Fakenham – and was now an expert in his field. He and Herbert Coleman each drove a Burrell's lorry to Chipping Sodbury quarry. Colonel Cleaver knew that these men were experienced engineers and asked them to stay and work for him, which they did. Bert Norman is with his steam roller, watched by Hedley Newman – perhaps at Poole Court for the local show?

Pontin's workrooms, in what is now the site of Yate Windows, *c.* 1925. These tailoring workrooms were run by 'Juby' Pontin until he moved to Tresham. Juby Pontin and his assistant Dicky Dixon, on his right, are at the back. It was later run by Mr Hawkins and his twin daughters, Iris and Ivy, as well as their elder sister, Ethel, also worked there.

Gilbert Shipp was a chimney sweep but also had a small farm in North Road. He had several brothers and, as children, they lived in a small cottage near Goose Green. From left to right: Brian Shipp, Gilbert Shipp. Middle row: John Osborne, Helga Osborne, John Thorncroft, Maureen Thorncroft. Back row: Rosemary Payne and -?-.

The Parnalls began business in Bristol in 1820. They made weights and measures and constructed shop fittings and shop fronts. In 1898, they were bought out by W. & T. Avery, but the firm still carried on in the Parnall name. With their expertise in construction and woodworking skills, they turned to making aeroplanes during the First World War. In 1925, George Parnall resigned and set up in his own business. He came to the site of the Air Ministry maintenance base in Yate, which was ideal for the construction of aircraft and had being lying empty since the end of the First World War. It had an engine room, repair shops, spacious buildings and a small aerodrome. He began the design and manufacture of civil and military

aircraft and also repaired damaged planes. Work was carried out for, amongst others, Fairey Aviation Supermarine Flying Boats as well as Hawker and Gloster Aircraft. The erecting shop shown is, in fact, at their Coliseum works in Bristol during the First World War. Towards the end of the Second World War, the factory changed its name to Parnall Yate Ltd and began the manufacture of household appliances. Today it is known as General Domestic Appliances Ltd, with only a section of the Belfast roof remaining from the original buildings (for more information see *Parnall In Memoriam*, published by the Yate District Oral History Project).

This light aircraft, made by Parnall's, was forced to land just inside the market, still some 150 yards from the airfield. This happened in the mid 1930s and the men gathered around are probably factory workers from Parnall's. Fortunately, the pilot walked away unharmed.

Newman's factory started in 1932 when A.J. Newman and his younger brother, Hedley, moved from Bristol to Yate and set up a business repairing second-hand electric motors. The site was purchased by their father for £7,000 and initially called Newman Sons & Company, but in 1936 became Newman Industries, employing forty people. During the Second World War, they built new electric motors, tools and shells. The factory closed in 1988, before being purchased by Safeways and demolished shortly afterwards.

Christmas at Newman's and the children are assembled in the canteen before the tea begins, 1940s.

Newman's Christmas party, late 1940s. Jelly, biscuits and cakes seem to be on the menu.

Local farmers and their wives posing at the Yate cattle market in the early 1920s. The market, at the end of Station Road by the railway line, later became the site of the egg-packing station.

Stuart England with his first prize for a Hereford cross-steer (which weighed in at eighteen and a half hundredweight), Christmas 1957. It received the best price of £300 in the fat-stock show.

Yate Cattle Market, 1950s. Eileen Weaver (née Pritchard), from Oxwick Farm, is holding the sheep whilst members of the clergy watch. The Revd L.V. Wraith, third from the left, was rector at St Mary's church from 1948 until 1961 and was later buried in the churchyard.

Yate Market, c. 1960. With their prize-winning cattle, the three Febry brothers – from left to right: Fred, Bert and Joe – seem very pleased with the judge's decision.

During the Second World War, Mr Boulton's daughters worked on Elmgrove, their farm, which was in Church Road on the site of the Heron offices (see page 26). Mr Boulton was the headmaster of St Mary's School, following the retirement of Gaffer Brown. Miss Ann Boulton is driving the tractor and Miss Ruth Boulton is standing behind.

The last work team mining spar, or celestine (strontium sulphate). This is a very rare mineral and Yate has the largest-known deposits in the world. The mineral is extracted by open cast mining and much of the Yate area was mined before the modern developments took place. It was initially used to refine sugar beet and has more recently been used in the electronics industry. At first it was dug by individuals and farmers and the first recorded mining was in 1875. In 1912 it became a notable industry when the Bristol Mineral and Land Co. Ltd was founded. This continued to operate until 1969, when it was bought by English China Clay Ltd. Here are the last workers in Brookmead, Hall End Farm, March 1991. From left to right, are: Paddy Scannel, Tom Lynskey, Bob Dudley, Martin Scannell and Michael Scannel.

Six

Commerce

Powell's cycle shop in Station Road at the junction with Sunnyside Lane. This card was written on 17 October 1907, announcing the arrival of a baby boy into the Powell family. The baby was to be called Percival Gordon Powell. The postcard was written by Ernest Powell, to his aunt in Ilfracombe.

The middle of Station Road and 'X' marks the oldest house: this has now been modernised. The shop, to the left, was previously owned by Mr and Mrs Redman and is now a cycle shop. Note that there were only fields on the right-hand side of the road when this photograph was taken.

The girls get together outside Redman's shop, late 1890s.

No. 1, Jubilee Terrace, North Road. These cottages were built around 1898 to celebrate the Diamond Jubilee of Queen Victoria in 1897. Most of the other cottages have been demolished, but this one remains on the trading estate by the junction with Millbrook Road. The general store sold vegetables and antiques but is now a house, like the other remaining cottages in the terrace.

The general store at No. 1, Jubilee Terrace, North Road, 1947. This was run by Mrs Osborne (née Fletcher) and her son, John.

Derek Holbrook married a Belgian lady during the Second World War. They met when he was fighting in Belgium – he was a young man of nineteen and Gilot was seventeen. After the war, Derek worked in the building trade but gave it up due to ill health. He then went into partnership with Arthur Haines and ran two fish and chip shops in Yate, one in a house in North Road, the other in a wooden ex-army hut in Westerleigh Road, the cooking all being done by coal. Derek can be seen with his son Gregory outside the Westerleigh Road premises (above). In the 1950s, Arthur Haines left the partnership and Derek bought a grocery shop in Station Road. He purchased it from Mrs Smith and Miss George and made it into a fish and chip shop. With further extensions we can now see Pisces today opposite B & Q (below).

The dainties shop in Station Road opposite Newman's canteen, 1940s. The proprietor, Mrs Smith, is on the left and with her is the assistant, Miss George. The building has now become Pisces takeaway shop, owned by Mr Holbrook.

Looking down Station Road at the beginning of the century, we can see that the business names have changed but the buildings look remarkably similar to today. The road is very quiet – perhaps it is a Sunday? The shop to the right of the post office is Boulton Bros, the family butchers.

It was said that Mick Lane made the best lardy cake in Yate – having an inch of toffee in the bottom. Lane's market bakery was by Parnall's main gate and supplied rolls, sandwiches and cakes to the factory workers.

This was originally a First World War canteen, used by RAF personnel who were stationed at Poole Court. It then changed to a Christadelphian chapel, one of its members being Miss Fox from Yate House. It later still became a general store – J. Twidale and I. Hawkins are in the doorway. Finally, it was burnt down.

The Co-operative Society shop in Station Road, on what is now the site of Dillons. Opened in 1928, it replaced the old wooden hut that was in Eggshill Lane. The store moved from this site to the shopping centre in the mid-1960s.

Forrest's bakery and the post office in North Road (opposite Mission Road and next to the Baptist chapel), 1926. Note the post-box near the shop entrance. Mr Forrest JP, was later succeeded in his shop by his son, Eddie. His younger son, Jack, became a headmaster. The post office was later moved to Bert Roache's shop near the British School. The girl by the shop door is Rose Dyer and the girl with the bicycle is Joan Janes. Archie Mainstone is with his bicycle, by the chapel.

Elmtree turnpike house was situated close to what is now the car park to the White Lion and adjacent to the new development known as Turnpike Close. In the 1770s, the miners got tired of paying the tolls and took down the gate and set fire to the elm tree on the opposite side of the road. This picture, from the 1930s, shows part of the building being used as a shop, run by Mr Francis. He sold sweets for a halfpenny to the school children from the nearby St Mary's School. Mrs Underdown was the last resident. The building was pulled down to make way for redevelopment in the 1960s.

R. & W. Febry's yard, adjacent to the old gasworks. This was formerly the site of Bennett's ironworks. Two brothers, Dick and Bill Febry, ran coaches and lorries from this yard, which was opposite to the cow mills' car park. The Sodbury Queen was the name of the coaches. The yard was demolished and houses built in what is now known as Bennett's Court.

The first post office in Yate, located at the west end of what is now the site of the leisure centre. It was opened in the late 1800s and closed in the early 1900s and was run at one time by two sisters, the Miss Raggatts. During and after the Second World War, it was used to house refugees. It was eventually demolished to make way for redevelopment.

The new shopping centre. In 1960, the site was designated for development and this is how it looked near to the Swan Inn.

The extension to the shopping centre, under construction in 1980. This provided facilities for eleven extra shops and the Tesco superstore.

Seven
Personalities and Fashions

Martha Prior (1845-1925). She was born as Martha Warner at Warren Farm, Yate, and died at Oxford House in Station Road. On the death of her husband, she continued a very successful business at the Cow Mills. Very deaf in later life, she used an ear trumpet – an item not mentioned in her very detailed will! Oxford House was built using pennant stone from Nibley Mill quarry.

A delightful study of three, well-turned-out, Yate gentlemen at the turn of the twentieth century.

Nurse Gertrude Godsell was a midwife in the area in the early 1900s. This may account for lots of ladies called Gerty in the area!

Mrs Annie Jordan and her sons at the turn of the twentieth century. She sits with her three sons, from the left: John (Jack), Clifford and Ernest. Annie was a regular worshipper at St Mary's church, a keen member of the Women's Institute and a founder member of Yate's Friends and Neighbours' Club. After her husband died, in the mid-1940s, she continued living in the family home in Station Road until 1968. She then went to live a few doors away with her daughter Ivy, who had left Birmingham to look after her. Ivy continued to look after her until she eventually went into Manor Park Hospital, where she celebrated her 100th birthday in January 1976. Sadly, Annie died in June the following year.

The small boy standing on the easy chair and his sister hang on to each other for the camera. They are dressed in their Sunday best – which was the fashion when the photograph was taken around 1900.

Mr and Mrs Warner with their daughter, Ruth, on the right, and son, Jacko, seated in the middle, late 1890s. Ruth, the mother of the small child, Bertie, later looked after Jacko following the death of their parents.

The wedding of Marion Nelson and Robert Taylor at St Mary's church in the early 1900s. The bridesmaids were Winnie and Grace Taylor. The baby on the front right is Joyce Stevenson (née Nelson) and the baby on the left is Joe May.

A boy with a curl, *c.* 1914. Bert Nelson, aged three, is the youngest of five brothers and a sister. He is dressed in a smock over short trousers with stockings and boots. The curl was probably produced with a hot curling iron.

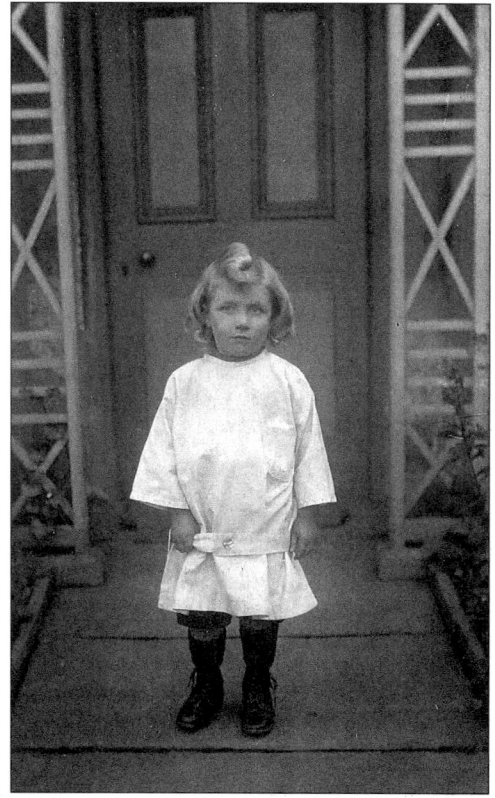

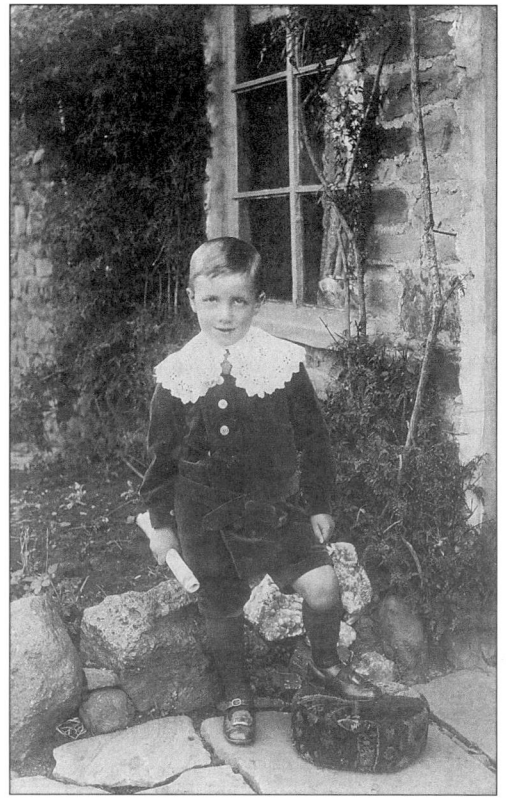

Bert Nelson, aged five, photographed by a travelling photographer, whose trademark was to have the subjects holding a scroll, *c.* 1916. The photograph was taken by a cottage in Westerleigh Road, behind a garden owned by the Church and currently the site of the petrol filling station.

Ruth Warner married Maurice Nelson in the late 1890s, and has been photographed by a travelling photographer in the cottage at Westerleigh. Note the stylistic device of a book held in one hand.

Four sisters, the daughters of Mr Hulands, the Yate undertaker, posing for the Edwardian photographer. Seated from the left: Alma, Pearl and Vida. Annie is the one standing.

Edward Griffin, shown right as a young man, lived in the Limekilns by Yate Court. He was captured by the Germans in the First World War and put to work on a farm. The photograph below shows him during his captivity, in a uniform provided by the Germans which was put on by successive soldiers whilst they were photographed. After the war he was reluctant to return home because of an attachment that he had formed with the farmer's daughter.

A delightful family group photograph of Mr and Mrs Herbert Haynes with their two children, Kenneth and Pearl, taken in the 1920s. Mr Haynes was a well-known horticultural judge.

In 1927, Mr Gibbins came to Yate from Bristol, with Mr and Mrs Walker, who had bought the Old Rectory. Mr Gibbins was their chauffeur and he and his family lived in the Old Rectory Lodge. In the picture, taken by the Old Rectory garden wall, are the four Gibbins boys. Leonard is in the hat (hugging his teddy bear), Desmond (popularly known as 'Tink') is wearing his tie, Raymond is the tallest one and Kenneth is behind Leonard. Mr and Mrs Walker sold the Old Rectory to Mr Hutson and so Mr Gibbins went to be Colonel Cleaver's chauffeur.

Bernard Skuse, or 'Tarzan', *c.* 1920. He worked as a building labourer and frequented the area, particularly around Bitterwell Lake. His son was Les Skuse, a tattooist in Eastville.

Mr Henry Ellison Nicholls, who lived at Goose Green Farm, with his horse, Whisky, at the Bath and West Show. He won many trophies for his expert horsemanship. Of all his horses, Amberley King was the champion.

Jimmy Dixon, *c.*1920. Jimmy was a local man who had two wooden legs following a railway accident. He used to undertake deliveries in the area, including regular errands from The George public house to Yate Railway Station.

Harold Lavis Williams, with the delivery lorry from Cow Mills, shown outside the two cottages (now demolished) opposite the White Lion, 1920s. The sacks of cattle food weighed two hundredweight and developed the muscles of the delivery men.

Edwin George Bacon was born on 8 August 1912 and served in the Red Cross during the Second World War. He was killed, by the Japanese, in Burma, during November 1944. He was the son of George Bacon, who was chairman of the Council from 1930 until 1936.

Councillor George Bacon JP, greeting His Grace the Duke of Beaufort at the opening of the parish hall on Saturday 27 October 1934. George Bacon (1887-1936), was a well-known figure in Yate, serving on no less than twenty-two committees and boards. These included being: a Justice of the Peace, Parish Councillor, president of the Chipping Sodbury branch of the National Railwaymens' Union, on the War Pension Committee, The Signalmens' Vigilance Committee, Guardian of the Poor and the founder member (in 1919) of the Fur and Feather Fanciers' Society. Above all, he was a Wesleyan Methodist lay-preacher. He came from Swindon to take up the post of signalman, at the Westerleigh West signal box, in 1908. Soon afterwards, he married Alice Smith and went to live in Jubilee Terrace. They had three children: Gertrude (now Mrs Higgins JP), Edwin and Cyril. He was instrumental in the building of Yate Parish Hall, where a clock in his memory can be seen today.

Mrs Bessie Bristow, the post lady, leaving Chipping Sodbury for Yate and Yate Rocks. This photograph was sent to her brother, Bert Febry, a prisoner of war in Germany during the Second World War. The stalag stamp is on the reverse of the original card.

Belgian refugees, Yvonne and Julian Arbon, arrived in Yate around 1941 and stayed here after the war.

Mr and Mrs Curtis (on the left) and Mr and Mrs Taylor, 1960s. Mr Curtis farmed Thorns Farm for Mr Hedley Newman and Mr Taylor worked for Bennett Ironworks. Mr Taylor went to live with his daughter in Australia when he was ninety. After his death in 1990, his ashes were sent home to Yate, where they were interred in St Mary's churchyard. The Yate District Oral History Project made a recording of the burial ceremony, which was then sent to his daughter, who plays it on the anniversary of his death.

Parish Councillors from around the 1930s and 1940s, from left to right: Mr Ranger (a builder), Mr Draper (headmaster), Mr West (railwayman), Mr Thompson (retired grocer), Mr Bacon – the chairman (railwayman), Mr Appleby (attendance officer), Mr Chambers (undertaker), Mr Nelson (railwayman), Mr Cox (farmer), Mr Sluter (council clerk).

Mr Randall Horder and his dog Charlie at the turn of the twentieth century. If a penny, covered by a biscuit, was placed on Yate Station Bridge, Charlie's trick was to fetch the penny without eating the biscuit, then run the length of Station Road back to his master at The Barton.

Mrs R. Horder with her son Maurice, who is holding her baby grandson, David. Maurice was saved from drowning in the Spar Pools by his brother Cyril. Sadly, Cyril died in this worthy action.

Eight

Schools

The girls at Yate National School (now St Mary's) are knitting socks, using four knitting needles, for soldiers in the First World War. One pair seems to be ready for wear. The school building was erected in 1855.

Empire Day and Mr F.F. Fox is addressing the children at St Mary's School, late 1890s. Mr Fox lived in Yate House, which he rented from the Randolph family. He had two sons, William and Richard, and a daughter, Francis. In 1911, when the Randolphs went to America, his sons bought Yate House. Mr Fox was a manager of St Mary's School and, in later years, his son Richard also became a school manager.

A classroom in the National School, *c.* 1910. The pupils, girls in white pinafores and boys with Eton-style collars, look very serious. They are sitting at wooden desks, the tops of which were operated by a small wheel to move them up or down. Notice the 'spy-window' in the door through which teachers and pupils could be observed.

Mr E.J. Brown – 'Gaffer' Brown, as he was known – was headmaster of St Mary's School from 1901 until 1934. He was always formally dressed at school, wearing a watch chain across his waistcoat. He was a strict disciplinarian but scrupulously fair. His cane stayed on his desk but was rarely used. He is standing outside the schoolhouse, which was also used by the visiting doctor and dentist.

Solemn faces for the school photograph by the old Church of England School (St Mary's), with the headmaster, 'Gaffer' Brown. This photograph was probably taken during the First World War. Back row, from left to right: Hulands, Wiltshire, Gould, Madge Gould, G. Francis, Kitty Marklove. Front row: Eric Hawkins, -?-, Joe English, M. Lumber, Bob Baker (son of the stationmaster).

The Houses of Parliament, 25 May 1949. Staff, pupils and parents of St Mary's School, together with members of St Mary's Youth Club. They are accompanied by the headmaster, Eric Boulton, and the Rector of Yate, Revd Lawrence V. Wraith. They are meeting their Conservative Member of Parliament, Sir Derek Gunston.

A sailors' hornpipe, performed during a concert at St Mary's School in the early 1950s. Amongst the pupils at the salute are: Judy George, Margaret Parks, Sheila Vick, Monica Nelson, Mary Southam, Pamela Lucas, Eileen Hedge and Winnie Griffiths.

Boys from North Road, or Yate British School, with Councillor Rogers, their headmaster, about to work in the school gardens, 1922. Mr Rogers was also the chairman of the Yate Parish Council.

Pupils and teachers from North Road School with farmer Mr Bruce Isaac at Hall End Farm, *c.* 1952. The boys were to have instruction on apple grafting.

Pupils from North Road School on their monthly visit to Hall End Farm for agricultural instruction. The tutor is Mr Christopher, from the Gloucestershire Agricultural College in Hartpury, and he is demonstrating the workings of an electric fence. In the front are Arthur Harford and Bernard Wooles.

Further instruction for pupils from North Road School in a field of corn, with Mr Bruce Isaac, the farmer, on the left and Mr Hayes, the teacher, on the right. The visible pupils, from left to right are: John Keedwell, John Painter, David Turpin, David Isaac, Geoffrey Bateman, Gordon Townsend, Harry Ramsey, Bernard Wooles, Vernon Gregory.

Presentation to Bruce Isaac, the farmer, by Mr Hayes, the schoolmaster accompanying the pupils from North Road School on their visit to the farm.

A mug to celebrate the start of free education on 1 September 1891. Mugs were issued to pupils by the Yate British School in North Road, this one being given to Jack Prout of Chaingate Lane. Up until this time, pupils had to pay a few pence each week for their education.

Aerial view of North Road School, which was built in 1850 at a cost of £375. The first headmaster was Mr Jacob Heglar. In 1879, it gained the status of public elementary school and received grants from the government. Mr William Parkinson was then the headmaster, assisted by James Iles (aged sixteen), who was monitor of Standard 1, Winifred Willis, monitress who taught the infants, and the seamstress, Mrs James Reed. When the nearby colliery closed in 1888, many of the families moved to South Wales. To help these people, sacks of bread, coal and clothing were handed out at the school, the money coming from an unknown source. The attendance of the pupils appears to have been very erratic, being influenced by the weather, Chipping Sodbury market, haymaking, potato picking, blackberry and hip collecting or illness. The registers were checked weekly by Mr Thomas Lawrence and prize money distributed by the Revd Pontifex to those who attended 400 times in a year! In the 1950s, a new secondary modern school was established in Chipping Sodbury and North Road School became known as Yate County Primary, no longer taking children over eleven years old.

The Ridge School staff, c. 1970. From left to right, front row: Mr Hill, Miss Smith, Mr Lewis (headmaster), Miss Holman, Mrs Nelson. Middle row: Mrs Bodkin, Miss Harris, Mr Evans, Mrs Higgins (secretary), Mrs Bullock, Mrs Fraser, Mr Bennett. Back row: Mrs Stone, Mrs Merrill, Mrs Draper, Mrs Denley, Mrs Tansley, Miss Snell.

Mr Howard Lewis. In 1954, the new Ridge Primary School opened in Yate and Mr H.C. Lewis became its first headmaster. He was very well-known, being chairman of both the magistrates' bench and Yate Parish Council. For his many services to the community, he was awarded the Queen's Silver Jubilee Medal. He served through the Second World War, and took part in the invasion of France on D-Day (6 June 1944). He eventually reached the rank of major. A fine sportsman, he excelled at cricket, becoming vice-chairman of Gloucestershire County Cricket Club.

Fancy dress at the Ridge School. This photograph was taken on the school field, showing the Terrapin classrooms in the background.

The centenary of the 1870 Education Act, which was the beginning of state education –whereby the provision of schools was not left to private charities. To celebrate the centenary, The Ridge School pupils staged a week-long Victorian exhibition. The contents of the exhibition were so valuable that, for insurance purposes, teaching staff had to be on site day and night.

Nine

Leisure

Enjoying a pint or two from their cider mugs, this happy gathering took place at the White Lion in 1919. Does the small trolley on the right belong to the little boy?

North Road band, early 1890s. On the left of the back row is Walt Pearce, with Harry Washbourne, a local publican, to his left. In the front row, on the left, is Mark Bateman from Roaches' shop, with Mr Watkins on the drum and Mr Livell from the Cider Mill in Dawes Lane on the right.

Yate British Band from North Road, c. 1910. 'The British' is the name of the lane between the school and the shop. It is suggested that the name derives from the time when there were both British and German miners working in the nearby coal pits. 'The British' was the name by which the local miners were known.

The Railway Hotel at the turn of the twentieth century. The ivy-clad hotel is located near to the station, ready to receive passengers before and after their journeys. In 1858, its host was a man called Robert Ford.

3 · A MEET OF FOXHOUNDS. – MR. NEIL'S, AT WHITE LION, YATE.

Tally ho! Mr Neil's fox-hounds meet at the White Lion, c. 1910. Some supporters have arrived by car. This postcard was sent to Miss Alison Barlow, who lived at Rodborough House, Clifton, in Bristol. The sender from Yate, who did not sign the card, writes 'Miss Lucy is on this somewhere' and 'Miss Lucy is in Bristol today shopping'. One wonders who this Miss Lucy was?

The rabbit and flower show in the Glen fields, *c.* 1900. Mr John Taylor Senior is third from the left.

The carousel: galloping horses in the early 1900s, with the steam engine generator pulled up alongside. This photograph was taken at Poole Court.

Yate Flower Show on 15 August 1907, with fairground amusements, at Poole Court.

An empty tennis court at The Lawns before the First World War (see page 18).

RAF Sports Day, 1919. Waiting for the start in the grounds of Poole Court.

Day trip to the coast, probably 1920s. Passengers include Mr Tily, Sergeant Davy and Mr Bethel (respectively the second, third and fourth behatted gentlemen from the left), as well as Mr and Mrs Williams and their son, Leslie, on the right.

The Garden Fête, *c.* 1928. Mrs Mabel Gibbins, from the Old Rectory Lodge, made flowers from silk and paper, giving demonstrations of this craft to local W.I.s and Mothers' Unions. In this photograph, Mrs Gibbins is handing a flower to the Dowager Duchess of Beaufort. Next to her is the Honourable Mrs Harford (from Horton Hall) and, on the far right, is Miss Fox from Yate House. This is the only photograph we have of Miss Fox, who went from Yate House to the Christadelphian chapel in Station Road by pony and trap every Sunday. One Sunday, as the driver, Jim Shipp, was passing the slaughterhouse – now the site of Fromeforde House – the horse smelt the blood and stopped dead. The strap to the trap broke, tipped it up and threw Miss Fox into the road. From then on she always travelled in a chauffeur-driven car!

Yate girl guides performing country dances in the Chipping Sodbury Pageant, held at Lilliput Court in July 1935. Margaret and Barbara Taylor are two of the dancers.

Yate Rovers, with the Yate YMCA in the background, 1921. From left to right, back row: Fred Baker, Wilf Taylor, John Wilcox, Syd Shellard, Len Perrett, Mr Dearden, Sid Sluter. Front row: Sid Nelson, Stan Hicks, Harry Baker, Ted Shellard, Frank Marklove, Sid Painter.

Ladies' football team, late 1930s. Yate ladies, in men's football gear, played football against the Yate men's football team, who wore fancy dress. They played on the aerodrome site, where B&Q is currently situated. The Yate team captain played in goal for the ladies. All proceeds were given to the Cottage Hospital. From the left: Eileen Armour, Gertie George, Dorothy Bevan, Ivy Hawkins, Gladys Anstee, Frank Boulton (captain of the men's team). Boy Gould (with cup), Betty George, Gladys Nicholls, Audrey James, Josephine Clements, Iris Hawkins.

Yate Football Club, 1933/34 season. From left top right, back row (standing): Cyril Fry, Alfred Baker, Wilf Taylor, Frank Boulton (who later played for Arsenal), Jim Boulton, Maurice Horder, Bill Reed (trainer). Middle row (seated): Don Wiltshire, Ted Horder, Ray Reed (killed outside his house by a bomb), Boy Gould (captain), Jumbo Boulton, Harold Wheeler, Cyril Bacon. Front row (on the ground): Edwin Bacon, Gilbert Wheeler, Vic Boulton, Harold Cox.

The 1948 league football team. The players, many of them recently demobbed from the services in the Second World War, played for Yate on their football pitch (which was where the swimming pool now stands). From left to right, standing: Mr Woodfield, Tink Gibbins, George Dudley, Bill Flynne, Len Woodfield, Jack Woodfield, Fred Nicholls, Eddie Flynne, Cyril Bacon, Mr Flynne. Kneeling: Fred Smoothy, Eddie Walters (?), Johnnie Washbourne, Bern Hicks, Stan Brindle.

Yate YMCA football team, 1949/50 season. This ground was more or less on the site of the present sports and leisure centre in Kennedy Way. From left to right, back row: Reg Fifield, Tom Tilling, Bill Flynn, George Dudley, Len Woodfield, Bill Febry, Frank Cook, Ben Appleby, Fred Nicholls, Terry Jordan, Eddie Flynn, Alf Maunder (district league secretary), Mr Woodfield. Front row: George Strange, Cyril Bacon, Taffy Jones, Jack Woodfield, Bern Hicks, Cecil Fletcher, Alfie Paul.

Yate YMCA football team, 1951/52 season. This side was later to become Yate Town Football Club, as the village grew into its present status. From left to right, back row: Fred Smoothy, Geordie Longstaff (referee), Ivor Dando, Frank Cook, Reg Skuse, John Dudley, Eddie Flynn, Les Nelson, John Sellick. Front row: Des Luton, Jack Walters, Jock Beveridge, Jack Woodfield, Bill Flynn.

Yate YMCA cricket team, c. 1950. From left to right, back row: Fred Nicholls, Reg Skuse, Bob Dudley, Terry Jordan, Graham Brain, Reg England (scorer). Front row: Trevor Townsend, Brian Tooth, Ivor Dando, Les Nelson, Jack Woodfield, Bob Jordan.

Player members of Newman's cricket team, in a road restaurant *en route* to Cardiff, 19 June 1967. From left to right: Maurice Gay, Pat Pinnigar, Clive Young, Reg England, C. Bryer, Bob Jordan, Rich Jordan, Sid Smith, Tony Scrivens.

St Mary's youth club party in full swing, during the early 1950s. From left to right, seated: Sheila Jordan, Jennifer Rose, Rosemary Underwood, Queenie Nelson, Bill Jones, Graham White. Standing: Raymond Avent, Richard Jordan, Tony Moulsdale, Peter Underwood, Roy Cheese, Arthur Wallington, Marion Taylor (in the kitchen).

Members of St Mary's youth club and friends, Christmas party, early 1950s. From left to right, front row: Mrs Gertie Nelson, Revd D. Brooks (Chipping Sodbury), Mrs Winnie Shellard, Mr Eric Boulton (headmaster of St Mary's School), Revd Lawrence V. Wraith, Miss Sheila Jordan, Mr Hector Chapel, Mrs Marian Taylor. Middle row: Barry Cooke, Rita Bedgood, Valda Amos, Barbara Shellard, Bob Jordan, Ruth Boulton, Jean Tazewell, Audrey Hill, Margery Watts, Queenie Nelson, David Underwood, Edith Hodkinson, Margaret Tazewell, Margaret Beard, -?-, -?-, Anne McGregor. Back row: Tony Moulsdale, Peter Underwood, Michael Gowan, Richard Jordan, Nigel Balchin, Brian Tooth, Tony Brown, Colin Hocking, Anne Boulton, Iris Walters, Mrs Brooks.

A ride in Cinderella's coach, *c.* 1955. Mr Alec Gifford is on the right of the ponies and Mr Roy Reed on the left. The ponies were owned by Mr Cavill, a deaf and dumb gentleman, who kept them at Stanshawes Court, or in the field by The Swan, where they were looked after by Mr Reed. The ponies and coach were used in pantomimes at the Bristol Hippodrome.

Martin and John Dowse feeding the ponies (in the field where the shopping centre is today), 1955. Sometimes the ponies were kept at Stanshawes Court. Cars are parked outside the White Lion on the right. The building in the middle is Elmtree Turnpike House. The left-hand side was owned by Mr Hawkins and the right-hand side by Mr Francis. Carlton House, to the left, was occupied by Miss Jones and was used as committee rooms during elections. The house has been awaiting renovation for some years. On the extreme left of the picture are some of the Barton Cottages, which were demolished when the shopping centre was built.

Carnival Day in the football field, 1960s. This has been held every year since the coronation of Queen Elizabeth II. The carnival queen on this occasion was the daughter of the landlord of the Beaufort Hunt, a public house in Chipping Sodbury High Street. Sally Tovey is the attendant, Mrs Pease is standing up in the second row and Mandy Higgins (now Dr Higgins) is the child on the right of the front row. John Heath can also be seen, surrounded by the girls.

The dart team's presentation makes for a happy scene in the White Lion in the late 1950s. The landlord, Mr Bert Pullin, on the right, is holding the cup with the help of the team's captain, Mr Bert Nicholls.

A proud moment for the delighted crowd of darts team members from the White Lion as they receive the Chipping Sodbury and Yate District Winners Cup. It is being presented by the league's president, Hugh Gray (on the left), to captain Wilf Taylor during the early 1960s.

A group of regulars having a quiet drink at the White Lion, 1960s. From left to right: Roy Senior, Doug Nelson, Julian Arbon, Sid Nelson and Fred Nicholls.

The start of the building of the leisure facilities, which began with the Southwold Sports Centre in 1970.

This humorous card was sent to E. Tucker Esq, Belvedere, Kent and postmarked July 1909. Part of the message reads 'It rained yesterday but is very nice today' – a nice sentiment on which to end this book